LOUIS ARMSTRONG

LOUIS ARMSTRONG

by Genie Iverson

illustrated by Kevin Brooks

THOMAS Y. CROWELL COMPANY
New York

CROWELL BIOGRAPHIES
Edited by Susan Bartlett Weber

Library of Congress Cataloging in Publication Data. *Iverson, Genie. Louis Armstrong. SUMMARY: A biography of the famous trumpeter from his childhood in New Orleans to the time when he was known as "Ambassador Satch" and "King of Jazz." 1. Armstrong, Louis, 1900-1971—Juv. lit. [1. Armstrong, Louis, 1900-1971. 2. Musicians. 3. Afro-Americans—Biography] I. Brooks, Kevin. II. Title ML3930.A7519 788'.1'0924 [B] [92] 76-4975 ISBN 0-690-01127-X*

3   4   5   6   7   8   9   10

LOUIS ARMSTRONG

Louis Armstrong poked his head out from behind Grandma Josephine's long dress. He was playing hide and seek with the boys who lived in the big house where Grandma worked.

Grandma washed and ironed for white folks in New Orleans. She brought five-year-old Louis with her when she came to work.

As she leaned over the washtub in the backyard, Louis felt her body sway. She moved in time to the sloshing sound the clothes made as they were rubbed up and down on the washboard.

Louis liked to play here in the big yard. Sweet-smelling magnolia trees shaded the garden, and the grass was damp and cool between his toes.

Across town in Louis' neighborhood, there were no cool lawns. He lived in a crowded, broken-down section of New Orleans called "back o' town" with many other poor black families. He was born there on the Fourth of July, 1900.

Louis and his friends played barefoot in dirt lots littered with broken glass and rusty tin cans. They chased each other through boarded-up buildings, abandoned but not torn down.

Louis lived with his mother, Mayann, and his younger sister, Beatrice, in a room near Perdido Street. He hardly remembered his father, who was divorced from Mayann.

Mayann cooked for a white family. She worked hard but earned barely enough to buy food for her family.

When Louis was seven, he began selling newspapers after school. The pennies he earned helped buy red beans and rice for Mayann to cook.

From his newsstand, Louis watched boys steal bananas and oranges from street vendors' carts and market stalls. Often they picked fights with each other just to have something to do.

Mayann worried that Louis would get into trouble, too. She told him time and again not to steal. "It's not right and it's not necessary," she said. "What's for you, you'll get."

While Mayann worked, Grandma took care of Louis. If she caught him fighting or gambling, she sent him to cut a switch from the chinaball tree beside her house. "You've been a bad boy," she scolded. "I'm going to give you a good licking."

Once Louis brought back the tiniest switch he could find. Grandma laughed and let him off. But other times she whipped him for everything bad he had done for a week.

Sundays Mayann and Grandma took him to hear the minister preach.

"Don't lie. Don't steal. Don't pick fights," the minister warned. "That's where trouble starts."

Then the minister began to sing. The congregation joined in. Life was hard for people on Perdido Street but in church they sang about a better world to come. Louis knew the hymns by heart.

But the kind of music Louis loved most was jazz. Jazz was African drum rhythms, French and Spanish dance melodies, church music and work songs from the days of slavery, all mixed together.

Most black jazz musicians played from memory. Because their music wasn't written down, they could play the way they felt. They could add sad notes and happy notes, composing as they played. The music would be a bit different each time. They called it improvising.

Louis loved the way jazz wove different rhythms and melodies together. And the syncopated rhythm of the music, with the accent on weak beats, made Louis' feet dance.

Jazz bands played at picnics, dances, and church socials. When they marched through the streets, children and grown-ups followed them. Heads back and knees lifted high, they strutted in time to the music. Second liners, they called themselves.

Brass bands even played their new music at funerals. On the way to the cemetery they walked along slowly, playing solemn hymns. But on the way back they broke into loud, happy tunes. This music was for the living. Weaving back and forth across the road, they high-stepped into town to the beat of "When the Saints Go Marchin' In."

At night jazz poured from neighborhood honky-tonks and saloons, where people drank and danced and tried to forget their hard lives. Louis often hid in the shadows outside listening.

One night he crept inside a saloon where Joe Oliver, a famous New Orleans jazzman was playing the cornet. Louis sat down on the floor. Through the blur of dancers' legs, he saw Oliver press his shiny cornet to his lips and

blow. High jubilant notes filled the room. The dancers stamped their feet on the floor and shouted for more.

Louis sat spellbound. "If I had a horn," he said to himself, "that's the kind of music I'd make."

On hot summer nights Louis and his friends swam in the Mississippi River. Afterward, they stretched out on the dock and sang the songs they heard in the honky-tonks.

When Louis was twelve, he and three boys organized a singing quartet. Louis could always hear a wrong note.

He made the boys sing each song over and over. Finally he decided they were good enough to sing in public.

It was almost dark on Rampart Street. The dance halls were open, and Louis heard the tinkle of piano music. Standing under a street lamp, he and his friends began to sing.

Slowly a crowd gathered. People in nearby buildings opened shutters and leaned out.

Louis danced a jig, whipped off his cap, and bowed. The crowd cheered and tossed coins into his cap.

After that, the boys sang every night. They divided their money, and Louis ran home to give his share to Mayann.

When the boys were on the streets late at night, they kept a sharp lookout for the police. For a long time they stayed out of trouble, but then Louis' luck ran out.

It was New Year's Eve. Firecrackers were exploding all over New Orleans. Roman candles whistled through the dark sky overhead.

Louis wanted to celebrate, too, He took an old revolver from the bottom of a trunk where Mayann kept it hidden. Slipping it under his shirt, he raced outside to his friends.

He could hardly wait to surprise them with his giant noisemaker. "Watch me!" he shouted. He whipped out the revolver and fired it over their heads.

Two strong arms grabbed Louis. Squirming and kicking, he looked up into the face of a policeman. "Please mister, don't arrest me," he begged. "I won't do it no more."

That night Louis slept in jail. Next morning a policeman led him outside to a horse-drawn wagon.

"This way," the policeman ordered. "You're going to the Colored Waifs' Home for Boys."

The heavy door slammed shut, and the wagon rolled out of the police yard. Louis squeezed his eyes shut to hold back the tears.

Life at the Waifs' Home was strange and frightening. On Perdido Street Louis had been able to come and go as he pleased. At the Waifs' Home he had to live by rules.

He and the other boys went to bed early, got up early, ate meals, and went to classes when the bugler blew his horn.

If Louis wasn't in the mess hall when the bugle blew

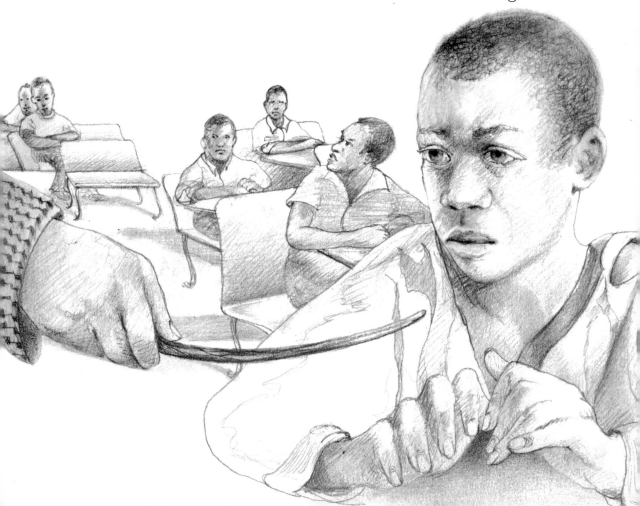

at mealtime, he missed his meal. If he whispered in class after the bell rang for silence, he was whipped.

The music teacher, Mr. Peter Davis, caught Louis breaking a rule during the first week. "You're one of those bad boys from Perdido Street," he said. He thrashed the palm of Louis' hand until tears splashed down the boy's cheeks.

Mornings the boys studied arithmetic, reading, and spelling. Afternoons they learned gardening, carpentry, or music.

Boys in the music class belonged to the Waifs' Home Brass Band. On weekends Mr. Davis took them into New Orleans to play in street parades.

Louis longed to be in the band. But he didn't dare ask Mr. Davis.

Evenings when the band rehearsed in the music room, Louis sat outside. He pretended he held a cornet. He pressed the imaginary valves up and down in time to the music.

As the weeks went by, Louis tried to stay out of trouble. Finally Mr. Davis asked him to join the band.

Louis learned to play the tambourine and the drum. Then when the boy who played the bugle was sent home, Mr. Davis gave Louis the chance to take his place.

Every day Louis practiced. He learned to control his breath so that he could blow clear, even notes. Within a week he was sounding all the bugle calls.

The boys liked the happy way Louis made his bugle sing. They also liked his big, easy smile.

"You got a mouth as wide as an open satchel," one of his friends said. "I'm going to call you Satchelmouth."

The nickname caught on.

At last Mr. Davis handed Louis a cornet.

Louis cradled the battered horn in his hands. It was the most beautiful thing he had ever seen.

Mr. Davis taught Louis to grip the horn's mouthpiece tight with his lips. He told him that practice would make his lip and jaw muscles strong.

The cornet was hardly ever out of Louis' hands after that. High notes, low notes, glad notes and sad notes, he played them all.

"Louis," Mr. Davis said, "I'm going to make you leader of the band."

The next time the band marched in a street parade in New Orleans, Louis was up front blowing his horn. When they swung down Perdido Street, old friends jammed the sidewalk. They cheered as Louis high-stepped past in his band leader's uniform. Louis' mother and sister cheered, too.

After a year and a half at the Waifs' Home, Louis was sent back to his family. He was fourteen now and could blow a horn as well as many of the grown men in New Orleans. He quit school and set out to find work as a cornet player.

His first steady job was at one of the city's toughest honky-tonks. Gamblers and thieves went there. They drank too much. Tempers exploded. Bullets and broken bottles shot past the bandstand.

But Louis wasn't afraid. He was being paid to blow his horn.

The owner didn't pay much though. Only fifteen

cents the first night. When Louis' sister found out, she laughed. "Huh," she said. "Blowing your brains out for fifteen cents."

Louis had to get a second job. From early morning until after dark, he drove a mule cart through the streets and delivered heavy sacks of coal.

Sometimes he stopped outside the cabaret where Joe Oliver was playing with one of New Orleans' most famous jazz groups. It was called Kid Ory's Band. Through the open windows Louis heard the wail of his hero's horn.

Word of Louis' cornet playing spread. Curious, older jazz musicians came to hear this teen-ager blow.

One night Joe Oliver walked into the saloon where Louis was playing. Louis saw him over the rim of his cornet. His heart pounded, but he managed to swing smoothly into his solo.

Louis began to improvise. His excitement could be heard in his music. Higher and higher he climbed on the scale. When he reached high C, he held it longer than he ever had before.

The room exploded with applause and cheers. Oliver pushed his way to the platform and shook Louis' hand. "They told me you was good," he shouted. "I just had to hear you. What you got, boy, brass lips?"

Louis soon was spending time at Oliver's home. Oliver gave Louis lessons, and they played duets together.

Oliver gave Louis one of his old cornets. It's been mighty good to me," he said. "You take it from here."

When Oliver went to work in Chicago in 1918, Louis took his place in Kid Ory's Band. Now he was heard in New Orleans' best hotels and cabarets.

Louis' next job was with Fate Marable's Band on a riverboat. They played for passengers and people living in towns up the Mississippi.

The paddlewheeler slowly churned upstream. Cypress and cottonwood saplings hung over the river, almost hiding shantyboats and fishing barges tied up along the bank. Above the levee on either side stretched green fields of sugarcane.

Afternoons, the band rehearsed new music. Louis knew that the other members of the band could read the sheet music. He couldn't. Before he could try a new tune, he had to hear it played through once.

The musician next to Louis noticed this. "You can blow and you can swing because it's natural to you," he said. "But you'll never be able to swing any better until you learn to read. Want me to teach you?"

Louis was eager to learn. Each morning he studied the notes, lines, and spaces on the printed music. He soon was playing with a new confidence.

To travel on the Mississippi and play for dancers who loved jazz was a wonderful way to earn a living. Between trips he worked in New Orleans' cabarets. With his steel-hard lips and powerful lungs, he could now hit and hold higher notes than any cornet player in town.

When Louis was twenty-one, Joe Oliver invited him to join his band in Chicago. As leader of the group, Oliver played first cornet. Louis would play second.

Louis was excited but scared. Many musicians who went north hoping to become famous, hitchhiked their way home flat broke. As he packed his clothes into a cardboard suitcase, he wondered what would happen to him.

This was his big chance. Jazz was booming on the South Side of Chicago, where black people lived. It had been carried there from the South by black workers looking for jobs in Chicago's factories. Now its rhythms vibrated from nightclubs and dance halls, catching the

fancy of the whole city. White people went to the South Side night after night. They liked this free-swinging music from New Orleans.

Louis felt homesick at first among Chicago's gray-stone skyscrapers. Elevated trains rumbled above streets that were crowded with strange faces.

But at the big Chicago nightclub where King Oliver's Creole Jazz Band played, audiences loved Louis from the start. When he and Oliver played together, the wailing of the cornets blended perfectly.

"Hey," the people shouted at Oliver, "that boy will blow you out of business."

Louis was proud and happy to play with his old friend and teacher. He made records with Oliver and the band, and toured several states. Oliver treated him like a son, and Louis called Oliver Papa Joe.

But after two years, Louis grew restless. As second cornet, he followed Oliver's lead and improvisations. He had to hold back on his own improvisations and not outblow his teacher.

When another band offered him a job as first cornet, Louis accepted. Papa Joe understood. His student was ready to be on his own.

During the next six years, Louis played with many different bands in New York and Chicago. His solos won him new fans and fame.

At Roseland Ballroom, a dance palace in New York City, he played with the Fletcher Henderson Orchestra. Henderson was creating a new style of jazz for big bands called swing.

Louis left Roseland at midnight and hurried to Harlem, a section of New York where many black people live. There, in black nightclubs, he and other jazz musicians played together until dawn just for the joy of playing. They called it jamming.

Once at the Vendome Theater in Chicago, the band leader asked Louis to play a trumpet. Louis liked the trumpet's clear tone. And he liked its size—larger than his cornet. "From now on the trumpet's my horn," he decided.

Louis was singing now. He used his throaty voice like a horn. Instead of words he sometimes sang nonsense sounds like "skid-dat-de-dat." He called it scatting.

Louis began to make records, first with famous blues singers like Bessie Smith and then with his own groups—the Hot Five and the Hot Seven. The records carried the sound of Louis and his horn everywhere. Many said they were the best records of New Orleans jazz ever made.

Louis' solo improvisations grew longer and more daring. Each time he played a melody, he played around with it, making up the music as he went along. He blew loud and low-down. Then soaring, he tossed out high skin-tingling notes.

People felt laughter and tears coming through his horn.

Soon Louis was traveling around the United States with a band of his own. More and more people asked him to sing in his deep-down, gravelly voice. At the end of a song he mopped his face with the white hand-kerchief he always carried, threw back his head, and said, "Yeeaah!"

In Hollywood he made his first motion picture. Fans lined up at movie theaters to see and hear him.

Louis was thirty-one when he next returned to New Orleans. Eight brass bands welcomed him as his train rolled into the station. At the head of a noisy parade he rode through the streets where he had sung years ago for nickels and dimes.

A crowd of five thousand people waited for his performance at the Suburban Gardens nightclub. No black man had ever performed there before.

"A white man's place," Louis called it.

The concert was to be broadcast on radio for everyone to hear.

As Louis and his band took their places behind the stage curtain, the white announcer stepped to the stage.

"Ladies and gentlemen, we have with us tonight—" He stopped. "I haven't got the heart to announce that nigger on radio," he said and walked off.

The audience gasped in shock. Louis' fingers tightened around the neck of his horn. He was stunned, but he knew that cruel words must not stop his music.

He pushed the curtains aside and walked to the microphone.

The audience cheered. "Hurray, Louis!" they shouted over and over.

"Thank you, folks, thank you," he said. Then he waved the band into his theme song, "When It's Sleepy Time down South."

Like many black people, Louis had often been hurt by the unkind words and actions of white people. When he and his band toured from city to city, restaurants refused to serve them because they were black. Many times they weren't allowed to sleep in the same hotel where they performed.

Louis said, "To come from a concert where people are

cheering you and then be given the icy brush by a hotel clerk can hurt real bad."

Louis toured states where people believed black and white musicians should not play together. Some states had even passed laws against it. Louis had black and white musicians in his band. He hoped people would decide the law was wrong when they saw and heard his men playing side by side.

"We bring contentment and pleasure," he said. "It's bound to mean something."

In 1942, Louis married a beautiful dancer—Lucille Wilson. Lucille knew that music would always be the most important thing in Louis' life.

"I love her because she understands that," he said. "She's on my side."

Louis' horn was heard around the world. He traveled from country to country with his newest band, the All Stars.

Wherever he went, he spoke the language of friendship and music, and people everywhere understood him.

Once from a stage in London, he bowed to the king of England who was sitting in the royal box. "This is for you," he said, and he played a song called "You Rascal You."

English fans shortened Louis' name from Satchelmouth to Satchmo. Fans everywhere soon were calling him Satchmo.

Louis became an ambassador of goodwill for the United States. Now when he toured foreign countries, he carried a message of friendship from people in America.

When his plane landed in Brazil, South America, firetrucks and police cars had to hold back thousands of fans who came to greet "Ambassador Satch." In Australia he gave twenty concerts in ten days, and every show was a sellout. And in West Africa half a million people packed a sports stadium to welcome their black brother from across the sea.

Touring day after day was hard work. Blowing his high notes often meant cracked and bleeding lips. He performed many times when he was exhausted and sick.

Young musicians listened to Louis and learned. They

called him the King of Jazz and the greatest trumpeter in the world.

When people listened to Louis, they felt close to him. They knew that when he improvised he was giving them part of himself.

"People say to me, 'What do I think of when I'm playing?' Well, I just think about all my happy memories and the notes come out. Always has been that way," Louis said.

As Louis grew older, his wife, Lucille, hoped he would rest and take care of himself. But Louis didn't want to rest. He was happiest when he was playing his horn and entertaining people.

"What's the good of having music in you," he asked, "if you can't get it past your pucker?"

Louis went right on making music until he died, two days after his seventy-first birthday.

He had lived doing what he wanted to do. He had shared the music and joy and love that he felt inside. "You understand," he said, "I'm doing my day's work. Pleasing the people and enjoying my horn."

ABOUT THE AUTHOR

Genie Iverson's writing career began when at eight she was the editor, publisher, printer, and reporter for a "short-lived one-page newspaper, posted on tree trunks." After her graduation from the University of California, Ms. Iverson worked for a few years as a newspaper reporter and feature writer. Now she is concentrating on writing biographies and history for children. About this book, she writes: "Louis Armstrong made me happy while he lived; he makes me happy now when I see him in my mind's eye and when I listen to his music—a heritage I value."

Genie Iverson lives in San Mateo, California.